Thinking About Reading

This page and the next will help you think about the kinds of books you read and how you read them.

What kinds of books have you read? Draw a line from the cover to a book on the shelf if you have read or looked at a book like it.

The thing I like best about books is _____

_____

A book I want to read is _____

_____

continued ▶

Self-evaluation   **Observation Option**—See end of book.   1

You know about these parts of a book. Which do you use to choose the books you want to read? Put a check mark √ in the circle.

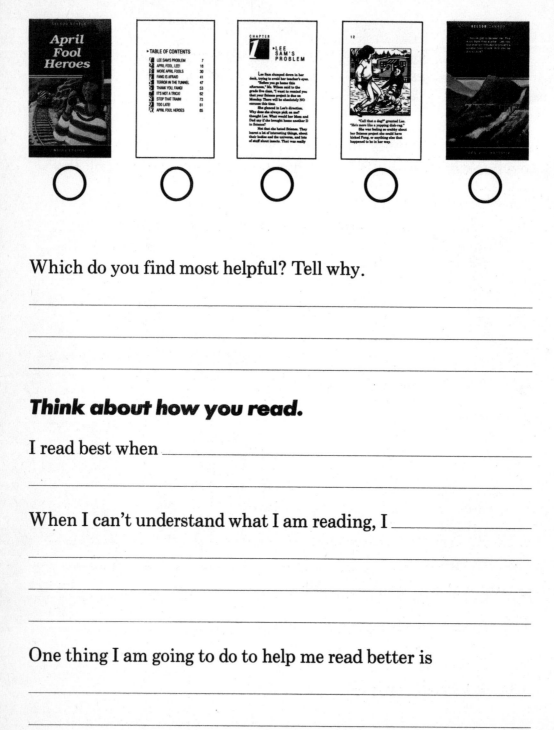

Which do you find most helpful? Tell why.

_____

_____

_____

Think about how you read.

I read best when _____

_____

When I can't understand what I am reading, I _____

_____

_____

_____

One thing I am going to do to help me read better is

_____

_____

I Want to Know

▶ **First** think of three things you would like to find out about.

▶ **Next** write three questions you would ask to get the information. Begin each question with one of the words in the box.

Who	*When*	*Why*	*What*	*Where*	*How*

1. _____

_____

2. _____

_____

3. _____

_____

Now choose two of your questions and write where you will look for the information. Put the number of your question beside your answer.

_____

_____

_____

Share your questions and answers with a partner.

Are You Curious?

One of the best reasons to read is to get information. Here is a chance to tell how you read for information.

▶ **First** look at the article on the next two pages.

▶ **Next** look at these different ways you can read an article:

  • Read the article from beginning to end.
  or
  • Read the headlines first.
  or
  • Read the parts that look interesting first.
  or
  • Look quickly through the article, then read it carefully from the beginning.
  or
  • Read the short parts first.

▶ **Now** read the article in any way you choose.

CELEBRATIONS

People often do special things on special days, and across the world there are many different kinds of holiday celebrations. Some are very old; others are fairly new. Some are serious; others are just for fun.

Bathtub Races

On July 1 people hold races in bathtubs between Vancouver Island and the British Columbia mainland. The first bathtub race took place in 1967 to celebrate Canada's 100th birthday. Now people come from all over the world to take part. More than 100 bathtubs are in the races.

Red Eggs

Red is the favourite colour for Easter eggs in many parts of Europe. Do you know why? Long, long ago, people believed that red was a magic colour. Some kinds of red berries were used to keep evil spirits away. The Chinese often gave each other red eggs at their spring festival.

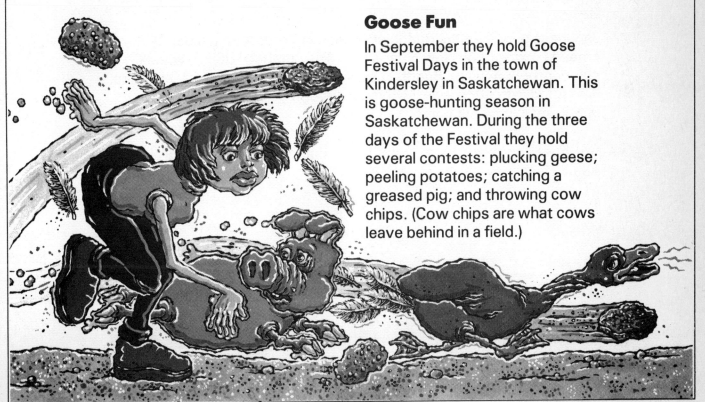

Goose Fun

In September they hold Goose Festival Days in the town of Kindersley in Saskatchewan. This is goose-hunting season in Saskatchewan. During the three days of the Festival they hold several contests: plucking geese; peeling potatoes; catching a greased pig; and throwing cow chips. (Cow chips are what cows leave behind in a field.)

continued ▶

Canada Day "Dip in the Bay"

Every year there is a relay race in Churchill, Manitoba on July I. The last runner has to jump into Hudson Bay. The temperature of the water is usually no more than 10°C - brrrr! The day also includes games, contests, a parade, a food fair, and a dance.

Discovery Day

Do you know how St. John's, Newfoundland got its name? It is called St. John's because the explorer John Cabot sailed into the harbour there on the eve of St. John's Day in 1497. In Newfoundland, St. John's Day on June 24 is now a holiday called Discovery Day.

Bells

Japanese people of the Buddhist religion in Toronto ring a bell 108 times at midnight on New Year's Eve. The number 108 is a special number for Buddhists. Buddhist prayer beads always have 108 beads. And Buddhists often walk 108 times around buildings that are important in their religion.

▶ **Now** tell how you read the article. Look back at the list of ways on page 4.

_____

_____

_____

Talk with others about the way you read articles for information.

▼▼▼▼▼▼
The Three Robbers

> **S**tory maps help readers understand stories. This page will give you a new look at "The Three Robbers."

▶ **First** look over the story map.

▶ **Next** write what you know about the characters at the beginning of the story. You may want to read "The Three Robbers" again before you start. You may also want to talk about the story with a classmate. Then write the ending in the last box of the story map.

The Characters

The Three Robbers   **Tiffany**

_____

_____

_____

▼

The Events

1. The robbers stop the carriage in which Tiffany is riding.

2. The robbers take Tiffany to their hide-out.

3. Tiffany asks what the robbers' treasure is for.

4. The robbers buy a castle with their treasure.

5. Lost and unhappy children come to live in the castle.

6. The children grow up and build a village.

▼

continued ▶

The Ending

_____

_____

_____

_____

▶ **Now** write something new you learned about the story from the map.

_____

_____

_____

_____

Story maps can help you write your own stories.

8

▼▼▼▼▼▼▼

How Do You Know?

*H*ow can you figure out what a new word means? One good way is to use the context—that is, the other words and sentences around it.

▶ **First** read each group of sentences.

▶ **Next** look at the underlined word in the group. Which of the three words underneath gives its meaning? Put a check ✓ in the box beside your answer.

1. Once upon a time there were three fierce robbers. They went about hidden under black capes and tall black hats.

☐ friendly   ☐ very tough   ☐ silly

2. The first robber had a blunderbuss. The second had a pepper-blower. And the third had a huge red axe.

☐ thick scarf   ☐ bad cold   ☐ heavy weapon

3. The robbers' hide-out was a cave high up in the mountains. There they carried their loot. They had trunks of gold, jewels, money, watches, wedding rings, and precious stones.

☐ valuable   ☐ purple   ☐ large

▶ **Now** underline the words in each group that helped you figure out your answer.

Talk with a partner about the ways you figure out what new words mean.

Words Have Feelings

*M*any words have a special "feel" to them. Say the word "blunderbuss" three times. It's a pretty heavy word, isn't it? Here's a chance to think about feelings words give you.

▶ **First** say all the words in the box out loud.

plundered	*flit*	*oaf*	*hobnob*	*squeegee*	*befuddled*
squirt	*twirl*	*crumb*	*hopscotch*	*egg*	*wiggle*
squash	*tiptoe*	*squelch*	*oboe*	*galoshes*	

▶ **Next** look at the webs on this page and the next.

▶ **Now** add the words to the webs where you think they belong. You may want to add the same word to more than one web.

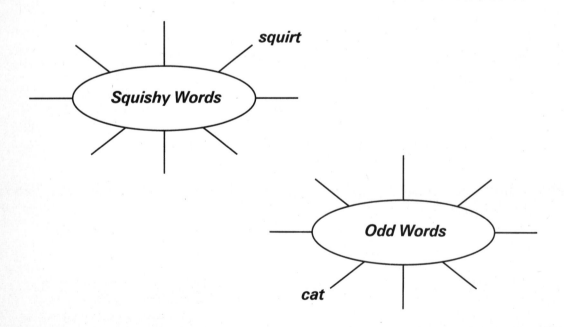

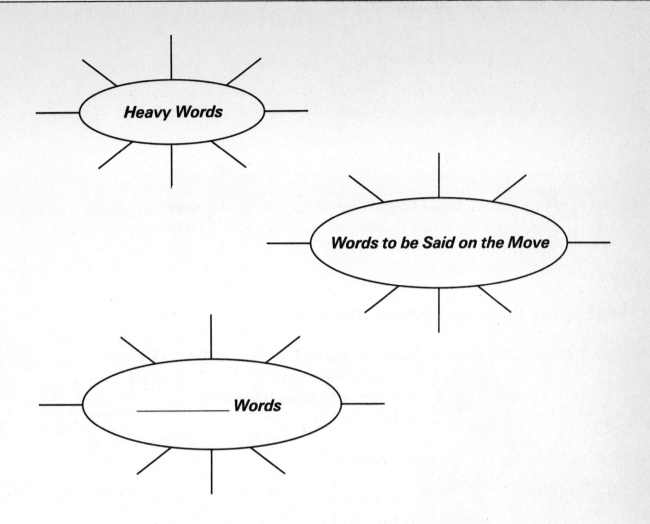

Do you have to know the meaning of a word to add it to a web?
☐ yes ☐ no

Can the sound of a word help you guess its meaning? Why do you think so?

_____

Words like "whirr" and "crack" sound like what they mean.

Think of another word that sounds like it means. _____

Think of other words to add to the webs.

Say the words in the webs out loud with a partner. Did you agree on where the words belong?

What the King Didn't Know

> **K**ing Henry and John Cabot had different ideas about Newfoundland. This page and the next will help you think about different points of view that people have.

▶ **First** think about the selection "What the King Didn't Know."

▶ **Next** write what you think the people are saying to themselves.

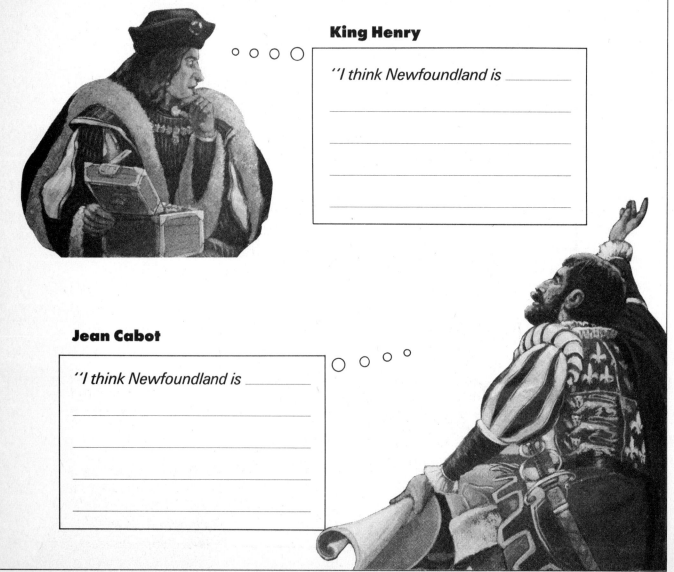

King Henry

"I think Newfoundland is _____

_____

_____

_____

_____

Jean Cabot

"I think Newfoundland is _____

_____

_____

_____

_____

Why does the king have a different point of view from John Cabot? _____

_____

What would you think or feel about Newfoundland

1. if you were a Newfoundland fisherman?

''I think Newfoundland is _____

_____

_____

2. if you were a tourist hiking across the island?

''I think Newfoundland is _____

_____

_____

Talk with a classmate about your answers.

13

Comparing Stories

> *H*ow are the three "Stories to Solve" alike? How are they different? Comparing stories helps us learn how stories work.

▶ **First** look at the chart. Read the headings and the words in the boxes at the top.

▶ **Then** write notes in each column for each story. You can use the words in the boxes at the top or your own words. You may like to work with a partner.

Story Name	Characters	Style of Writing	Why Author Wrote It
	• people • animals • have names • described in detail	• short • long • lots of details • lots of action	• to entertain • to give information • to make a puzzle
Fishing			
A Drink for Crow			
Which Flower?			

Write a story of your own. You can use a chart like this to help you plan it.

Words Make the Connection

W*riters use many different words together in sentences. This page will give you practice using some of these words.*

▶ **First** look at the words in the chain.

and | but | where | because | until | so that | even though

▶ **Next** read the sentences below.

▶ **Now** choose words from the chain to complete the sentences. You may use some words more than once. It may help you if you read the sentences aloud or with a partner.

1. Two fathers and two sons fished _____ talked all morning long _____ by noon everyone had caught a fish.

2. As the two fathers and the two sons walked home, everyone was happy _____ each had a fish _____ only three fish had been caught.

3. A crow flew down to a pitcher _____ he had gotten a drink of water the day before, _____ there was only a little bit of water.

Talk with a partner about these connecting words. Why are they important? Explain why you chose the words you used.

Cloze (Function Words)   ***Observation Option**—See end of book.*   ***Stories to Solve***

Let Us Perform for You!

LISTENING-WORKSHOP ACTIVITY

You can perform a reading of the poem "Chant." Decide who the lucky audience will be. Then use this page and the next to plan and practise your reading.

▶ **First** listen to a reading of the poem "Chant."

▶ **Next** read the poem aloud with your classmates several times.

▶ **Next** decide who will read each of the lines. Write the name of the reader beside the line. You may want to read some lines as a group. Write "All" beside these lines. Underline the lines that you will read.

▶ **Now** try different ways of reading and presenting the poem. Make notes beside the lines. You may want to add music or other sound effects.

Reader	Chant	Notes About How We Will Read
	by David McCord	
_____	The cow has a cud	
_____	The turtle has mud	
_____	The rabbit has a hutch	
_____	But I haven't much	
_____	The ox has a yoke	
_____	The frog has a croak	

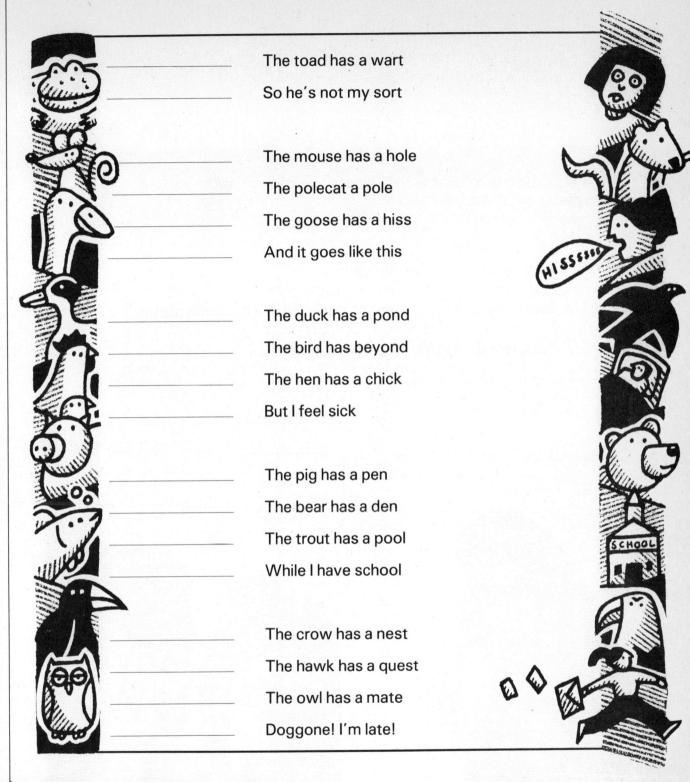

The toad has a wart

So he's not my sort

The mouse has a hole

The polecat a pole

The goose has a hiss

And it goes like this

The duck has a pond

The bird has beyond

The hen has a chick

But I feel sick

The pig has a pen

The bear has a den

The trout has a pool

While I have school

The crow has a nest

The hawk has a quest

The owl has a mate

Doggone! I'm late!

▶ **Now** practise performing the poem. When you are ready, present your reading to your audience.

Make a tape of your performance to play to other audiences.

Give Them a Voice!

What if animals could talk? This page and the next will let you put words in their mouths.

▶ **First** look carefully at each photograph.

▶ **Next** brainstorm sayings on a sheet of paper or with a classmate.

▶ **Now** write the animals' words in speech balloons.

Bird Talk/The Tree Frog

Composing (Speech Balloons)

Choose one picture. Did your words make the picture funny or
did they make it serious? _____
Try writing a new speech balloon that changes the meaning.
Why are the words that go with pictures important?

_____

_____

_____

*Share your animal
sayings with your
classmates.*

The Clever Turtle

Good readers are always thinking ahead as they read. This page and the next will show you how well you think ahead.

▶ **First** read the story below.

▶ **Next** fill in the blanks with words that make sense. You may find it helpful to read the sentences aloud with a partner.

One day a man left his village to look after his field of corn.

But he _____ only empty space where the _____ corn had stood. He saw a turtle _____ in the sun. He caught the turtle and _____ it back to his village.

The man and the people of the _____ decided to punish the _____. First they said "We should _____ him for stew." The turtle said, "I'd make a _____ turtle stew, but, *please* _____ throw me into the river."

Next the people decided to _____ the turtle to a tree. The turtle said, "Do anything, but *please* don't _____ me into the river."

Then the people thought of putting the turtle in a hole. The turtle said, "Dig the hole deep, but _____ don't throw me into the river."

The Clever Turtle　　*Observation Option—See end of book.*　　*Cloze (Retelling)*

So the _____ threw the turtle into the _____.

The turtle said to them "I was born and bred in a _____ bed. You just couldn't get the best of me!"

▶ **Now** answer these questions.

1. Did you find it easier to predict the words at the beginning of the story or toward the end?
   ☐ At the beginning   ☐ Toward the end   ☐ Both

2. Why do you think that was so? _____

_____

_____

3. What things do you do to make predicting easy as you read?

_____

_____

_____

_____

Talk with a partner about ways to become better at predicting. Try out your ideas on something you are reading.

Telling Stories

Some story ideas are so good that people use them over and over in different ways. Here's a chance to take an old story idea and use it in a story of your own.

▶ **First** read the story map of "The Mean Old Mean Hyena" on this page and the next. You probably know this story already.

▶ **Next** look at the story map for "The Clever Turtle." You have just read this story in your Anthology. Complete the story map.

The Mean Old Mean Hyena

The Clever Turtle

The Beginning

The mean old mean hyena played tricks on the zebra, the elephant, the ostrich, and the lion.

The Beginning

A man discovered that his new corn had been ruined. He saw a turtle dozing in the sun.

The Middle

The animals caught the hyena. They wanted to punish him. They thought of different ways to do this. They talked about knocking him, socking

---

The Middle

The man caught the turtle and took it back to his village.____

_____

_____

him, beating him, and eating him.

The hyena said the animals should do what they wanted with him. They could punch him, pinch him, or pickle him. "But," said the hyena, "please, don't tickle me!"

The Ending

So the animals tickled the hyena. The hyena called them fools. He said he loved nothing more than laughing. How he laughed as they tickled him.

So, in the end, the hyena wasn't punished at all.

The Ending

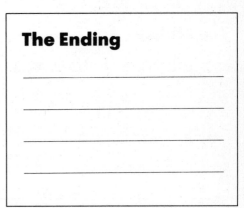

▶Next think about how the stories of the hyena and the turtle are alike. Then brainstorm ideas for a story of your own with the same pattern. Use the webs below to help you.

1. Who gets caught?

2. What did the bad guy do?

3. Who catches the bad guy?

4. How does the bad guy trick everyone?

continued ▶

► **Now** put your ideas together in a story map.

The Beginning

_____

_____

_____

▼

The Middle

_____

_____

_____

_____

_____

_____

_____

_____

▼

The Ending

_____

_____

_____

_____

Make a note about this story in your Writing Folder. You may want to publish it later.

24

A Pride of Lions

We often use special words to talk about groups of animals—for example, a flock of geese or a pack of wolves. Here's a chance to play with this idea.

▶ **First** look at the cartoon below.

▶ **Next** choose *two* of the animal group names in the box below and draw a cartoon for each. Write the name of the group below it.

a pod of whales	*a bed of oysters*	*a cry of hounds*
a band of gorillas	*a school of fish*	*a murder of crows*

_____   _____

Composing (Representing)   ***The Clever Turtle***

Is That a Hat?

Look at the words in the box on this page. Decide where on your body you would wear each piece of clothing. Write the word under the correct heading in the drawing on this page. If you don't know a word, look it up in a dictionary.

pork pie	suspenders	ascot	pullover	parka
panama	scarf	stetson	pince-nez	windbreaker
bowler	boater	monocle	beret	bonnet	anorak
cardigan	deer stalker	glasses	pillbox	blazer

• **Around the Neck**

• **On the Head**

• **Over the Shoulder**

• **For the Eyes**

• **On Top**

Sid the Rat

Vocabulary (Language Fun)

The box below gives you words you can list under the headings on this page.

sneakers   sash   slippers   trousers   belt
sandals   jeans   pumps   loafers   kilt   thongs
knickers   moccasins   runners   culottes   cut-offs

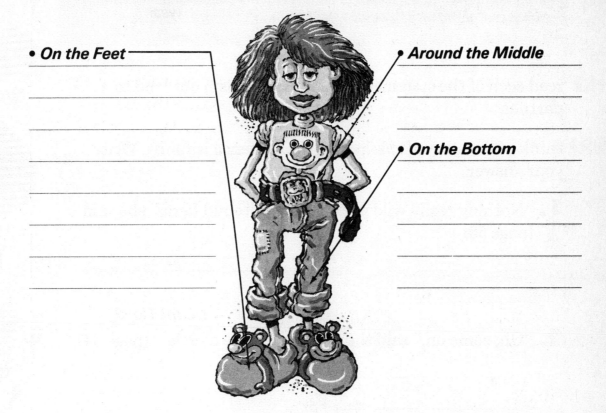

• **On the Feet**

_____
_____
_____
_____
_____
_____

• **Around the Middle**

_____
_____

• **On the Bottom**

_____
_____
_____
_____

Draw pictures of some of the pieces of clothing and label them.

What's So Funny?

You don't have to tell a joke to be funny. This page will help you think about one of the ways James Marshall made "Wings" funny.

▶ **First** read each of the statements below. Read them out loud to a partner.

▶ **Next** think of the story. Explain why the sentence is funny. Write your answer.

1. "Nothing really wild ever happens around here," she said. (page 53)

_____

_____

2. "Oh, come on," said the stranger. "Live a little." (page 54)

_____

_____

3. "Plump is nice," said Mr. Johnson. (page 54)

_____

_____

▶ **Now** talk about your answers with your partner. Find other lines in the story "Wings" that you thought were funny.

Tell Me Another One!

*D*o you think Harriet and Winnie would like chicken jokes? Here's a page of chicken jokes. Perhaps you can add to it.

▶ **First** match the questions and the answers. Draw a line between the question and the answer.

1. How long do chickens work?

Because talk is cheap.

2. What do chickens serve at birthday parties?

Around the cluck.

3. Why is it easy for chickens to talk?

She was tickled to death.

4. What do you get if you cross a chicken with an elephant?

A strange hen-encounter of the bird kind.

5. What happened to the chicken whose feathers all pointed inwards?

An egg big enough to feed an army.

6. What do you call it when you meet an eggs-tra-terrestrial?

Coop-cakes.

Do you know a chicken joke? Write it here and share it with a classmate.

_____

_____

Riddles (Language Fun)   *Wings*

Stone Age Facts

WORKSHOP ACTIVITY

*W*hat was life really like long ago when people lived in caves? We all wonder. Here's a chance to use your background knowledge and your common sense to figure out what could be true and what couldn't.

Working Alone

Read the story of the stone age family below. *Underline* anything you think could be true. Cross out everything you think is false.

The Thor Family

The Thor family was used to eating meat, berries, and eggs. They were also used to going hungry. Whenever Ma Thor heard that a new shipment of food was in at the market, she saddled up the Thor's sturdy stegosaurus and headed into town. Pa Thor stayed at home to tend the fire. Keeping warm in the winter was difficult and important. Meanwhile, the little Thors were busy with chores and schoolwork. They were especially happy thinking of the dinner to come—sizzling mammoth meat, a big bowl of nuts, and fresh oranges.

The Cave Boy   *Observation Option—See end of book.*   *Critical Thinking*

Working Together

Talk about the story of the Thor family with a group of your classmates. Then complete the sentences below.

1. We all agreed that _____

_____

2. What we disagreed on was _____

_____

Some of us thought _____

_____

Others thought _____

_____

Working Alone

Use your own knowledge and common sense to write a Stone Age puzzle paragraph. Write at least two things that are true and two things that are false.

_____

_____

_____

_____

_____

_____

Working Together

Challenge your group to spot the things that are false.

▼▼▼▼
Finding Facts

When you write a report, you need to read for information. This page will give you practice finding facts.

▶ **First** read each question below.

▶ **Next** look for answers in "Wild and Woolly Mammoths" in your Anthology. Below each question, write the first three words of the paragraph in which you find the answer.

1. What did woolly mammoths look like?

_____

2. Why did the dinosaurs die out?

_____

3. Who was the woolly mammoth's greatest enemy?

_____

4. Why are there no woolly mammoths alive today?

_____

▶ **Now** look at these strategies for finding facts in an article. Check ✓ the ones you used.
I skim the article first. ☐
I look for key words. ☐
I look for pictures of the information I need. ☐

Which strategy do you find most useful? _____

_____

Plant a Word

Words can grow like plants. From one root word you can grow many different words. All you have to do is feed it with beginnings and endings.

▶ **First** look in "Wild and Woolly Mammoths" for two words you can make from the word *hunt*. Write these words on the branches of the *hunt* plant below. Think of other *hunt* words you can make. Add these to other branches. It may help to work with a partner.

▶ **Next** write words you can grow from the root *trap*.

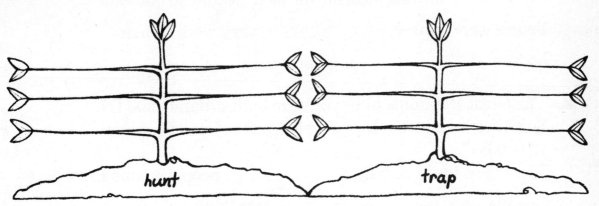

▶ **Now** find another word in "Wild and Woolly Mammoths" with a root word in it. Make the plant grow by writing other words with the root word in them. Use a dictionary—or make guesses.

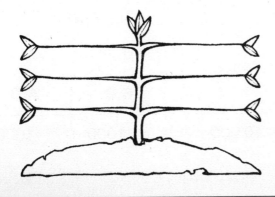

Play the plant game with a partner. See who can make the most words from a root word.

What Happened First?

People use numbers to show when things happened in history. These pages will help you understand what the numbers tell us.

▶ **First** read the sentences in each section below.

▶ **Next** use the words *before* or *after* to complete the first blank in each section. Use numbers to complete the next two blanks.

1. People began to live in villages and grow crops for food around 8000 B.C.
People were hunting animals for food around 30 000 B.C.

People were hunters _____ they were farmers,

because _____ is greater than _____ .

2. The Great Pyramids in Egypt were built around 3000 B.C. Scientists have proof that people lived in Canada around 13 000 B.C.
The Pyramids were built _____ people settled in

Canada, because _____ is less than _____ .

3. The first Olympic Games were held in Greece in 776 B.C.
Workers began to build the Great Wall of China in 214 B.C.

The Great Wall was built _____ the first

Olympics, because _____ is less than _____ .

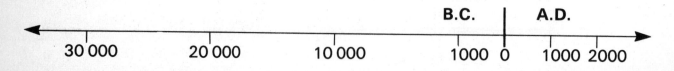

Wild and Woolly Mammoths   *Across the Curriculum (Mathematics, Social Studies)*

▶**Now** figure out how long ago these events happened. The information on page 34 will help you.

Example

How long ago did people begin growing crops for food?
People began growing crops around 8000 B.C.

To find how many years ago:
1. Take the number of years B.C.—   8000
2. Add on the year we are in—   <u>1990</u> (for example)
3. Add the numbers together—   9990

People began growing food 9990 years ago, or about 10 000 years ago.

How long ago did people first hunt for food?

1. _____

2. _____

3. _____

How many years ago were the Pyramids built?

1. _____

2. _____

3. _____

How many years have people been living in Canada?

1. _____

2. _____

3. _____

▼▼▼▼

Create a Beast

"A Prehistoric Who's Who" shows you one way to write information about animals. You can use it for ideas to write about a "prehistoric" beast of your own.

▶ **First** imagine your prehistoric beast. Ask yourself questions to help you picture it.

Will it be large? Small? Hairy?
Will it be scary? Funny?
What will it eat?
Where will it live?
How will it move?
Jot down your ideas in the space below.

A Prehistoric Who's Who   *Composing (Representing)*

▶ **Next** draw a picture of your beast. In the space below your drawing, write about the animal. Give it a name. Perhaps you can show how to say its name, as the author did in "A Prehistoric Who's Who."

Name of animal:

_____

_____

_____

_____

_____

Share your drawing with your classmates. You could make a "Prehistoric Who's Who" book of your own.

Stone Age Crossword

Here's a crossword puzzle that uses words from the "After the Dinosaurs" Theme.

▶ **First** read the words in the box below.

▶ **Next** read through all the *Across* and *Down* clues on this page and the next. Then use the clues to fill in the crossword with words from the box. Do the easy ones first. You can go back later to do the ones you skipped.

> **north   mammoths   scientist   tusks   mammal   stone**
> **prehistoric   planteater   Siberia   swamps   dinosaurs**
> **enemy   hot   cave   trap   pit   sea   hunter   flesh**

Across

1. Very, very old; before history began

— — — — — — — — — — — .

5. Ice is cold; fire is __ __ __ .

6. People were the mammoth's greatest __ __ __ __ __ .

8. Basilosaurus lived in the __ __ __ .

9. These wild, woolly beasts lived during the last ice age.

— — — — — — — —

12. Trappers catch animals in a __ __ __ __ .

13. Wet marshy lands are called __ __ __ __ __ __ .

16. A person who studies science is a __ __ __ __ __ __ __ __ __ .

18. These large reptiles became extinct 64 million years ago.

— — — — — — — — — .

Down

1. Brontotherium was a __ __ __ __ __ __ __ __ __ .

2. A person who hunts is a __ __ __ __ __ __ .

3. Cave people made tools of this. __ __ __ __ __

4. The opposite of south is __ __ __ __ __ .

7. The mammoth, like the whale and people, was a __ __ __ __ __ __ __ .

10. Elephants and mammoths have long, curved __ __ __ __ __ at the sides of their trunks.

11. Where a mammoth's body was found in 1901

__ __ __ __ __ __ .

14. What animals and people have on their bones __ __ __ __ __ .

15. Early peoples used to dig a __ __ __ to catch large animals.

17. Prehistoric people often lived in a __ __ __ __ .

Journey with Scarface

LISTENING ACTIVITY

To be able to marry Singing Rains, Scarface has to travel to the Lodge of the Sun. On this page and the next you can travel with him.

▶ **First** listen to "The Legend of Scarface."

▶ **Next** look at the paths on this page and the next. Think of the story. See if you can lead Scarface along the right path to the Lodge of the Sun and then back home.
Draw arrows →→→ to show your route.

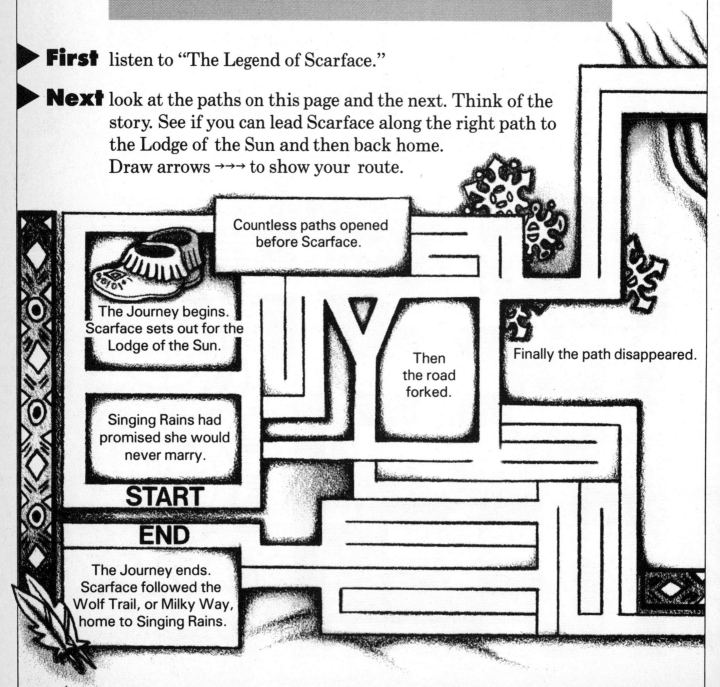

Countless paths opened before Scarface.

The Journey begins. Scarface sets out for the Lodge of the Sun.

Then the road forked.

Finally the path disappeared.

Singing Rains had promised she would never marry.

START

END

The Journey ends. Scarface followed the Wolf Trail, or Milky Way, home to Singing Rains.

Storyteller

Story Mapping

Scarface found a path filled with sweet perfume.

Scarface showed Morning Star the lost quiver.

Scarface travelled to the edge of the forest.

Morning Star led Scarface at last to the Lodge of the Sun.

Morning Star disobeyed his father. Scarface fought the fearsome birds.

Scarface was offered a reward.

How did you figure out which path to take? Explain to a partner how you did it.

41

My Journey

M*any good stories are about great journeys. Use this page and the next to help you plan a journey story.*

▶ **First** look over the planning questions on these two pages. Think about a journey story you would like to write. The picture on pages 94 and 95 of your Anthology may give you some ideas.

▶ **Next** use the planning questions to help you plan your story. You may want to use the space on the next page to draw the path of your journey as you plan your story.

Planning Questions

Who are the main characters?	Why do they need to make a journey?

▼ ▼

The Journey
Where do they go?
What persons or things do they meet?
What happens to them along the way?

▼

How does the journey end?

Use the space below to draw the path of the journey. You may want to add notes or speech balloons.

Talk about your story plan with another writer in your class.

▼▼▼▼▼▼
Reading Between the Lines

Janet and Richard showed their feelings in the letters in "The Southpaw." How do they feel now that Janet is on Richard's team?

▶ **First** read the questions in the interview with Janet.

▶ **Next** write answers that you think Janet might give to the questions.

▶ **Now** write another question for the interviewer and an answer for Janet.

An Interview with Janet

INTERVIEWER: Janet, you had a tough time getting on Richard's team. Why was that?

JANET: _____

_____

INTERVIEWER: How did you feel while you were fighting for a position on the team?

JANET: _____

_____

INTERVIEWER: How do you feel about Richard now?

JANET: _____

_____

INTERVIEWER: _____

_____

The Southpaw *Composing (Inferring Character)*

JANET: _____

_____

▶ **Now** do the same for this interview with Richard.

▶ **An Interview with Richard**

INTERVIEWER: Richard, the Mapes Street team got off to a rocky start this year. Why was that?

RICHARD: _____

_____

INTERVIEWER: Now that the girls are improving your season, how do you feel about girls as ballplayers?

RICHARD: _____

_____

INTERVIEWER: How do you feel about your friend Janet now?

RICHARD: _____

_____

INTERVIEWER: _____

_____

RICHARD: _____

_____

Share your answers with a classmate. Ask if the answers sound like Janet and Richard. Explain how you knew what to answer.

Mapes Street Plays Preston Ave.

Baseball has a language all its own. This activity will let you play with baseball language and decide who wins.

▶ **First** look at the cartoon.

▶ **Next** write words in the blanks in the cartoon. You can use words from the box or words of your own. Then draw the last picture in the cartoon to show how the game ends.

> bunt   curve ball   safe   strike   knuckle ball   homer
> bases loaded   steal   single   line drive   second
> fast ball   first   fly ball   scouts   line-up   third
> pitcher's mound   home run   slide   home plate   slugger

IT'S THE BOTTOM OF THE NINTH. MAPES ST. IS OUT IN FRONT 5-4. PRESTON AVE. SCORED THREE RUNS IN THE EIGHTH. CAN MAPES STOP ANOTHER SCORING DRIVE?

The Southpaw

Vocabulary (Language Fun)

ONE AWAY...

TWO AWAY...

Start a collection of baseball words—or words from other sports.

Become a Sports Writer

*W*hat makes a piece of writing good ? This page will help you answer that question. On the next page you can try out some new writing ideas.

▶ **First** read each section below.

▶ **Next** reread "The Babe Makes His Point" on pages 104 and 105 of your Anthology. Find examples of each writing idea. Complete the sentences with the examples you find.

1. The author of this article doesn't always use the name "Babe Ruth." For variety he also calls him _____

and _____

2. The author uses a mix of long sentences and short sentences.
Here's a long sentence: _____

_____

_____

Here's a short sentence: _____

_____

_____

3. The author gives the reader interesting details. For example:

_____

_____

_____

A Baseball Scrapbook   *Observation Option—See end of book.*   *Composing (Critical Thinking)*

▶ **Next** think how sports writing is different from other kinds of writing. Write some of your ideas here.

_____

_____

_____

▶ **Now** describe a sports event you have watched or heard about or taken part in. Try using some of the writing ideas Charles Wilkins used in "The Babe Makes His Point."

_____

_____

_____

_____

_____

_____

_____

_____

_____

_____

_____

Share your sports writing with a classmate.

When you read an article, how can you tell what it's about? This page can give you some new answers to that question.

▶ **First** read the article on this page.

Bell booms a Jay pennant warning

Grand slam puts 'em back in the hunt

With one swing of the bat, George Bell put the Blue Jays back in the race for the American League Division pennant yesterday.

Bell's dramatic, grand-slam home run in the bottom of the ninth inning lifted Jays to a wild, 9-7 win over Texas. The victory sets up a showdown series, starting tonight, with Detroit Tigers, who are tied with Boston for the division lead.

☐ **Win over Rangers puts Jays back in division race. Page B1**

Bell's heroics put the Jays $6\frac{1}{2}$ games behind the division leaders.

At the same time, Bell, who has been in the doghouse with Blue Jays' management and fans all season, won his way back into their hearts. There were 34 400 fans on hand at Exhibition Stadium yesterday.

The win capped a terrific comeback by Toronto. Jays trailed, 6-0, in the eighth inning, but scored five runs. Texas got a run in the ninth to lead, 7-5, but Toronto loaded the bases, then Bell bopped his sixth career grand slam well up into the left-field bleachers.

▶ **Next** answer the questions below.

1. What is the article about? _____

2. Is the sport named in the article? _____

3. How can you tell what sport the article is about? _____

_____

_____

Underline the words in the article that told you what it was about.

4. Which of these strategies do you use to find out what an article is about? Check √ the ones you use.

• I skim the article before I read it. ☐

• I look for important words that I know. ☐

• I read the title and headings first. ☐

Find another newspaper report that doesn't mention the name of the sport—or write a report. Let your friends figure out what the sport is about.

Casey at the Bat

LISTENING ACTIVITY

*T*he poem "Casey at the Bat" describes an exciting sports event. This page and the next will give you a chance to show the poem in action.

▶ **First** listen to the reading of "Casey at the Bat."

▶ **Next** imagine that you have made a movie about "Casey at the Bat." You need a poster to advertise the movie. Use the space below to plan what you would put on the poster. You might think about such things as these:

What words would I put on the poster?

What picture or pictures would I show on the poster?

What person would I choose to play Casey in the movie?

_____

_____

_____

_____

_____

_____

_____

_____

▶ **Now** draw your poster in the space on the next page.

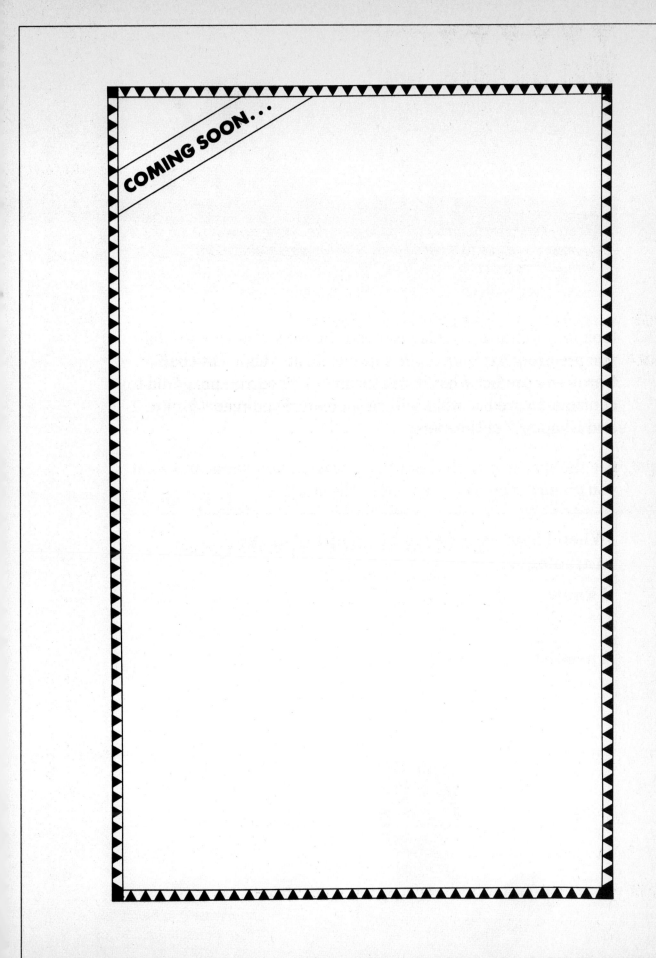

COMING SOON...

▼▼▼▼▼▼▼

What Will Happen Next?

Good readers try to predict what is going to happen next in a story. You can use these two pages and "The Magic Baseball Card" in your Anthology to practise predicting.

▶**First** look at the charts on this page and the next. You will see that you are going to preview the story of "The Magic Baseball Card" and predict what it will be about. Then you are going to continue to predict what will happen after you read Chapter 1 and Chapter 2 of the story.

▶**Now** use the spaces in each chart to write what you *know* and what you *predict* is going to happen in the story.

When I look over pages 112 and 113 of the Anthology...

I know _____

_____

I predict _____

_____

_____

Talk with a classmate about how you made your predictions.

The Magic Baseball Card   *Observation Option—See end of book.*   *Reading Process (Predicting)*

Now that I have read Chapter 1...

I know   _____

_____

_____

I predict   _____

_____

_____

Now that I have read Chapter 2...

I know   _____

_____

I predict   _____

_____

_____

▶**Now** finish reading the story. Then think about predicting. Write what you know about predicting in the spaces below.

1. Thinking about what I already know makes reading easier because

_____

_____

2. Thinking about what will happen next makes reading easier because

_____

_____

▼▼▼▼▼▼▼

I Can Make That Better!

*W*hy do good writers reread what they have written and make changes? Because they know that changing, or revision, makes their work more enjoyable to read. This page and the next will help you think about revising.

▶ **First** think about the changes you make when you reread something you have written. Answer the questions below.

1. What makes you decide to revise a piece of your writing?

_____

_____

2. What kinds of things do you change when you revise?

_____

_____

3. Do you like to revise as you reread your work? Why?

_____

_____

4. Why does reading your writing out loud help you make it better?

_____

_____

▶ **Next** look over the writing in the box at the top of the next page. Look at the changes the writer made. Then answer the questions below the box.

The Magic Baseball Card   *Observation Option—See end of book.*   *Self-evaluation*

> usually
> Snow was still on the ground here and there, *in ugly patches.* The wind
>
> would blow you right over or cut you in half if you weren't
>
> ~~was months from finishing.~~   happy
> looking. School ~~wasn't over.~~ But I was ~~glad~~ every March; *I was*
> happier   ever   Why?
> ~~more happy~~ than I felt on my birthday. Because I knew that
>
> soon the first pitch of the season would fly. Baseball was ~~a~~ *my*
>
> a kid.   It
> reason for living when I was ~~young~~ ~~and it~~ still is.

Do you think the writer's changes made the writing better?
Why?

_____

_____

Choose two changes that made the writing better. Explain why
you think they were good changes.

Change No. 1 _____

This was a good change because _____

_____

Change No. 2 _____

_____

This was a good change because _____

_____

▶ **Now** choose a piece of writing from your Writing Folder. Read it out
loud and make any changes that will make it better.

*Discuss a piece of your
writing with a classmate.
Let your partner help
you make it better.*

▼▼▼▼ Puzzle Page

Poets play with words. On this page and the next you can play with words and be a poet yourself.

▶ **First** read each of the word puzzles here. Read the words out loud. Listen to the patterns.

▶ **Next** add more words to continue the pattern.

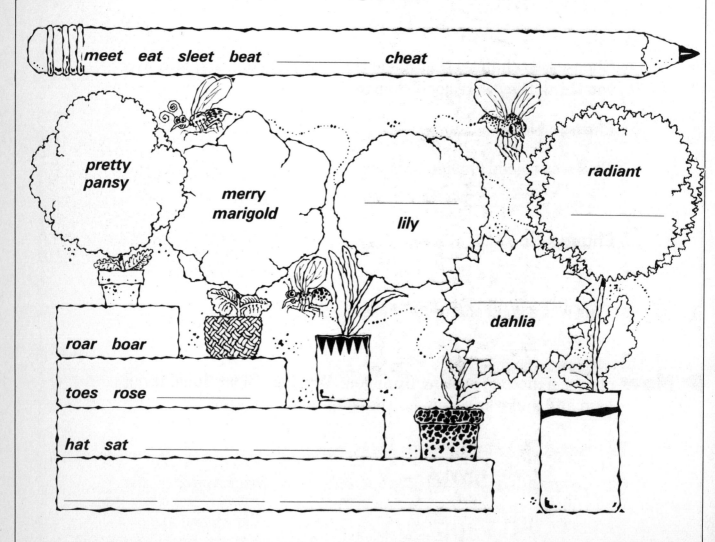

meet eat sleet beat _____ cheat _____

pretty pansy

merry marigold

_____ lily

radiant

_____

_____ dahlia

roar boar

toes rose _____

hat sat _____

_____

Eletelephony   **Observation Option—See end of book.**   *Vocabulary (Language Fun)*

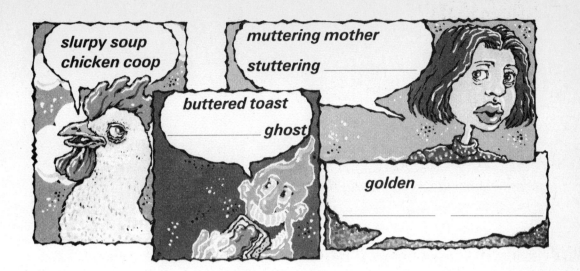

slurpy soup
chicken coop

muttering mother

stuttering _____

buttered toast

_____ ghost

golden _____

▶ **Next** tap or clap the words as you read this poem aloud. The missing
words will probably pop into your head. If they don't,
make guesses. Write the missing words
in the blanks.

As I was going out one day
My head fell off and rolled _____.
But when I saw that it was gone,
I picked it up and put it _____.

And when I got into the street
A fellow cried: ''Look at your _____!''
I looked at them and sadly said:
''I've left them both asleep in _____!''

▶ **Now** write a poem of your own. You can use words from the box or
your own words to make rhymes. Use another sheet of paper to
write your poem on.

bear	*chair*	*dare*	*fair*	*hair*	*care*	*scare*	*pair*
spare	*stair*	*stare*	*there*	*wear*	*square*	*swear*	
June	*loon*	*moon*	*noon*	*spoon*	*prune*	*soon*	*tune*
baboon	*balloon*	*harpoon*	*honeymoon*	*macaroon*			

How Do You Eat Peanut Butter?

*D*oesn't everyone like peanut butter? Here's a chance to look into that idea and practise using numbers.

▶ **First** study the chart below. Then use the chart to answer the questions on this page and the next.

City	Number of People Eating Peanut Butter			
	On a Bun	On a Roller-Coaster Ride	Off Their Elbows	In a Closet
St. John's	17 212	414	2	3 885
Montreal	75 627	6 811	0	11 016
Saskatoon	21 318	0	6	14 138
Victoria	13 789	4 739	1	8 532

1. How many people in Saskatoon enjoy peanut butter on a bun? _____

2. How many people in St. John's say they eat peanut butter in a closet? _____

3. What is the most popular way of eating peanut butter in all the cities? _____

4. What is the least popular way of eating peanut butter?

_____

5. In what city do the most people eat peanut butter on a roller-coaster?

_____

6. In what city can six people eat peanut butter off their elbows?

_____

▶ **Next** think of other places where people use charts to give information. List them here. _____

_____

Why do people use charts and tables to present information?

_____

_____

▶ **Now** make a chart of your own to show the following information about some favourite foods.

6 people in grade 4 like honey best.
7 people in grade 4 like peanut butter best.
10 people in grade 4 like jam best.
2 people in grade 5 like honey best.
20 people in grade 5 like peanut butter best.
5 people in grade 5 like jam best.

Give your chart a title.

More Puzzles

▶ **Look** over the puzzles on these two pages. Do them in any order you wish.

Crossword Towers - The Adventures of Isabel

Complete the first crossword tower. Then make up one of your own.

THE

```
1        A
    2    D
   3     V
 4       E
   5     N
6        T
     7   U
     8   R
 9       E
    10   S
```

Clues

1. Isabel ate this animal.
2. What Isabel did to the witch.
3. Very hungry.
4. A high-pitched noise.
5. To hit someone with your fist.
6. A very large fairytale creature.
7. A creature that says "Boo."
8. A big smile.
9. A kind of dry toast.
10. To frighten.

OF

| I |
| S |
| A |
| B |
| E |
| L |

Clues

1. _____
2. _____
3. _____
4. _____
5. _____
6. _____

Crossroads

Find any words that fit into the crossroads.

D		Q		S
R		U		H
A		I		O
N		E		C
K		T		K

Word Square

How many words can you find in this Word Square? The words can twist all around. You can use the letters more than once.
Hint: One word is GIANT.

C	G	R	N	E
A	E	A	N	T
R	B	E	W	O
G	L	N	T	R
I	A	D	R	Y

Make up some puzzles of your own. Share them with your friends or with someone at home.

Alphabet Crazy

WORKSHOP ACTIVITY

*P*eople have been making alphabet poems for hundreds of years. Here's a chance for you and your classmates to write an alphabet poem of your own.

Working Together

▶ **First** read the poems out loud. Read them again with a partner. Listen as your partner reads the poems.

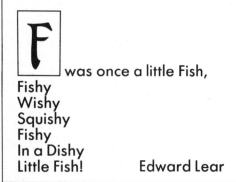
F was once a little Fish,
Fishy
Wishy
Squishy
Fishy
In a Dishy
Little Fish!   Edward Lear

O was once a little Owl,
Owly
Prowly
Howly
Owly
Browny Fowly
Little Owl!   Edward Lear

Talk about what makes the poems funny and clever. Write some of your ideas in the space below.

_____

_____

_____

_____

Composing (Conferencing)

Working Alone

Choose a letter of the alphabet and write a poem about it in the space below.

_____

_____

_____

_____

_____

_____

_____

_____

_____

Working Together

Read your poem to your classmates. Ask for suggestions to make it better. You can make notes below.

_____

_____

_____

Working Alone

Revise your alphabet poem. Or write another poem for another letter of the alphabet.

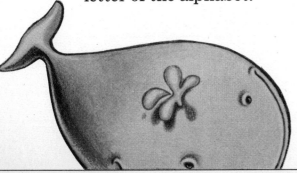

You may want to keep copy of your poem in your Reading Fun Folder.

Who's Telling the Story?

*T*he story "The Snake on Second Avenue" is written from the point of view of the boy. The boy lets you into his thoughts. On this page you can see how that's done.

▶ **First** look again at page 151 of "The Snake on Second Avenue" in your Anthology.

▶ **Next** find the words the boy uses that tell you he is the one who is telling the story.

▶ **Now** read the following part of the story. Think how it would sound if the boy's mother were telling the story.

"It's just a garter snake," said Mum, quite loudly. "It's not poisonous and it's not a constrictor. The only things it can damage are insects." She paused, then said, "And I'm going to take it home. Please excuse me." She didn't have to push her way out. The crowd just separated in front of her.

In the space below, write what the mother would say to tell this part of the story.

_____

_____

_____

_____

_____

▼▼▼▼
Book Talk

Read each card. Think of a book you have read or listened to that matches the words on the card. Write notes about it on the card. Practise telling other classmates about each book. Use the notes you made.

One book I thought was really great was _____ _____ _____ _____ by _____ _____ The reason I liked it was _____ _____ _____	A book that taught me a lot was _____ _____ _____ _____ by _____ _____ The reason I liked it was _____ _____ _____

Write a book tip to display on the bulletin board for your classmates.

▼▼▼▼▼
Not Ever Again

> **W**hen a story surprises or shocks you, it's a good idea to think it over. Making a story map can help you organize your thoughts about a story.

▶ **First** make a story map to remind yourself of what happened.

Characters	**Setting**
_____	_____
_____	_____
_____	_____

▼ ▼

Problem

_____

_____

▼

Events

_____

_____

_____

_____

_____

▼

Ending

_____
_____
_____

▶ **Now** write a short summary of the story. Use the story map to help you.

_____
_____
_____
_____
_____
_____
_____
_____
_____

Talk with your classmates about the story. How did you feel about it when you finished reading it?

Facts from Stories

> **S**tories often give us information as well as enjoyment. This page will show you some of the information you got from the story "Not Ever Again."

▶ **First** answer the questions below. You may want to look at the story in your Anthology to help you.

1. What makes it dangerous to go out on the ice, as Sonia did?

_____

_____

2. Why was it difficult for Sonia to swim or float in the water?

_____

_____

3. What things did the snowmobilers do to save Sonia?

_____

_____

4. What other things do you know about ice safety?

_____

_____

_____

Not Ever Again **Observation Option—See end of book.** *Skimming (Information)*
Composing (Representing)
Copyright © Nelson Canada, A Division of International Thomson Limited, 1989

▶**Now** draw a poster about ice safety. Use the answers you wrote on page 70 to help you.

Make a list of ice safety rules. Tape-record your list for others to listen

The Sparrow's Song

▶ **First** read this retelling of part of "The Sparrow's Song."

▶ **Next** write *two words* that make sense in each blank. You may want to read the sentences out loud to help you. You may also work with a partner.

Katie was fishing one day when a song sparrow splashed into

the water in a way that told her it was dead. Moments later, the

dead mother's baby _____ helplessly down toward her.

Katie _____ the baby bird into her fisherman's hat. Then

she turned and saw her brother Charles _____ a slingshot.

"It's only a _____," he said.

"And you're only a little boy," _____ Katie.

Katie raced away from her brother. Safe in her home, she

_____ the sparrow inside a cage. The frightened bird

_____ into a tight ball. Katie _____ it out, and

The Sparrow's Song

Cloze (Word Choice)

soon the bird _____ a bit of bread from her fingers.

Katie wanted the bird to fly, so she took it to the most magical

place she knew _____ to the mythic gorge. When she

and the sparrow sang together, their voices _____ like

sunlight off the walls of the gorge.

▶ **Now** show your work to a classmate. Compare the words you and
your classmate have chosen. Read the sentences aloud each way
to see which word sounds best in the blank.

*Finish retelling the
story of "The Sparrow's
Song" to a classmate.*

Looking at Both Sides

WORKSHOP ACTIVITY

Listening to different points of view helps writers. Here's a chance to talk with your classmates about animals and then write what you think.

Working Alone

Read each statement below. Check √ whether you agree or disagree, then explain why.

1. Everyone should have a pet. ☐ I agree ☐ I disagree.

_____

_____

_____

_____

2. People are more important than animals. ☐ I agree ☐ I disagree.

_____

_____

_____

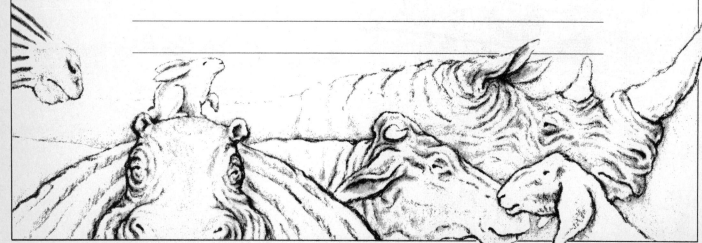

Working Together

Share your ideas about animals with a group of classmates. Listen to what they wrote about the statements. Make notes here of any new ideas you want to remember.

_____

_____

_____

_____

_____

Working Alone

Choose one of the two statements on page 74. Write a paragraph about it to persuade someone to share your point of view.

_____

_____

_____

_____

_____

_____

Sharing the Ark

The Theme "Sharing the Ark" probably gave you lots of ideas about animals. This page and the next will help you organize your ideas.

▶ **First** read all the idea webs on this page and the next.

▶ **Next** fill out the webs with your ideas. You may need to draw more lines from the web.

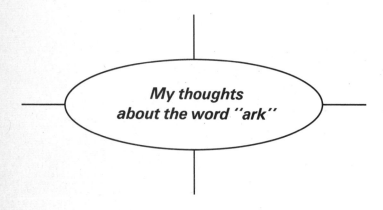

My thoughts about the word "ark"

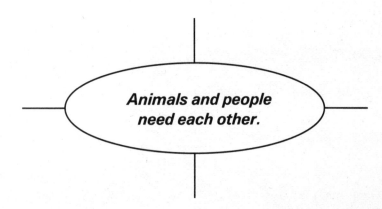

Animals and people need each other.

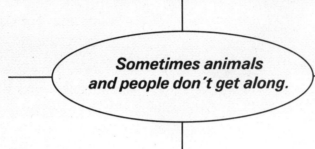

Sometimes animals and people don't get along.

▶ **Now** write what it means to "share the ark." How do you think people and animals should share our world?

_____

_____

_____

Talk with your classmates or people in your family about "sharing the ark" with animals.

77

Meet a Writer

AUTHOR AT HOME PERCHED AT HER WRITING POST.

*W**riters are usually curious about other writers. Here's a chance to learn some surprising things about a writer you already know—YOU.***

▶ **First** look over the interview with Patti Stren on pages 188 to 191 of your Anthology. What things in the interview did you find most interesting? Make notes of these things below.

_____

_____

_____

_____

▶ **Next** imagine that someone is interviewing you. Give honest answers to the questions, as Patti Stren does. You may be amazed at what you learn about yourself.

INTERVIEWER: What kinds of things did you like to do when you were a little kid?

YOU: _____

_____

_____

INTERVIEWER: When did you first start to be a writer?

YOU: _____

_____

_____

Meet Patti Stren   *Observation Option—See end of book.*   *Self-evaluation*

INTERVIEWER: Where do you get your ideas?

YOU: _____

_____

INTERVIEWER: Do you ever use people you know for characters?

YOU: _____

_____

_____

INTERVIEWER: What helps you most when you get the "blank piece of paper jitters," or "writer's block"—when you stare at the blank paper and can't get started?

YOU: _____

_____

_____

INTERVIEWER: What would you most like to tell readers about writing?

YOU: _____

_____

_____

_____

▶ **Now** read your interview. You may see things you want to change. You may want to add illustrations like Patti Stren.

Share your interview with other writers in your class. Ask if you can see theirs.

OBSERVATION OPTIONS

	Observation	**Facilitating Learning**
Thinking About Reading (pages 1-2) *Self-evaluation*	Do the children express opinions about their book choices? Do they demonstrate effective ways of choosing books? Do they have ideas about strategies for becoming more effective readers?	Encourage the children to discuss books and book choices with you, with classmates, with librarians, and with parents. Stimulate ongoing discussions about reading and writing strategies. Encourage the children to keep logs of their reading and writing and their attempts at trying new strategies.
How Do You Know? (page 9)	Are the children able to use surrounding text to infer the meaning of unknown or vaguely known words?	Provide many opportunities for the children to talk about words whose meanings are implied fairly clearly in the text, and opportunities to discuss with each other the creative ways they find of making these inferences.
Words Make the Connection page 15	Are the children aware of the importance of connectives as a means of understanding relationships between ideas when they are listening and reading? For communicating meaning as they speak and write?	Listening to and reading well-written text is probably the best single way of ensuring that children will develop a good sense of the *wholeness* of language, and wholeness demands an understanding of connectives.
The Clever Turtle (pages 20-21)	Do the children use strategies for prediction typical of fluent readers? Are they generally able to demonstrate fewer miscues later in a passage as a result of a context that has developed than from reading the first part (or listening to the first part read by someone else)?	Emphasize the fact that predictions do not generally involve "correct" answers, but rather ways of keeping the reader active in making meaning. For children who are having problems, it may be necessary to engage them in conference sessions where considerable modelling of predictive strategies occurs.
Stone Age Facts (pages 30-31)	Are the children developing awareness of strategies to read critically? Do they generally have the background knowledge to make such distinctions?	Workshop and conference sessions help children develop awareness that "paper never refuses ink," and that there are specific strategies to screen fact from fiction.
My Journey (pages 42-43)	Do the children demonstrate strategies for planning stories? Do they feel comfortable modifying these plans many times as they go about the process of composing?	Encourage the children to listen to and read well-written stories so they develop an ever-growing resource of story "echoes" in their heads. Children need much encouragement to spend time experimenting with various planning devices—talking to classmates, doodling, mapping, and combinations of these.
Become a Sports Writer (pages 48-49)	Are the children aware of the differences in style authors adopt for different purposes and different audiences, and can they apply this awareness as they interpret text when reading and listening?	Expose the children to a wide variety of writing styles. Discuss with them why authors decide on different formats and styles for different audiences and different purposes. Children should have the opportunity to listen for differences in "sound" and to recreate these differences as they interpret text orally.
What Will Happen Next? (pages 54-55)	Can the children make efficient use of information such as titles, illustrations, and opening paragraphs, and of discussion to develop a mental context for making sensible predictions about the text?	Develop concept webs *with* (not *for*) the children to help them access relevant prior knowledge they already have and to build on it. Encourage self-questioning, such as "What do I know about this topic, and what else would I like to learn about?"
I Can Make That Better! (pages 56-57)	Are the children aware that it is normal to make extensive revisions after the first or even the second draft in writing? Are they aware of the difference between revision and editing?	Exposure to quality literature is probably the best guarantee that children will eventually develop sensitivity to the need for revision. Model the need in your own writing, making clear that there is no such thing as a "correct" text. Emphasize the need for oral work in making decisions about revision.